Made in United States
Orlando, FL
21 May 2022

18065781R00061